DATA STRUCTURES AND DESIGN

BHARATHI S

TO GOD

Contents

CHAPTER ONE

Data Structures and Design will try to teach you about three things:

1. It will present a collection of commonly used data structures and algorithms. These form a programmer's basic "toolkit". For many problems, some data structure or algorithm in the toolkit will provide a good solution. We focus on data structures and algorithms that have proven over time to be most useful.
2. It will introduce the idea of tradeoffs, and reinforce the concept that there are costs and benefits associated with every data structure or algorithm. This is done by describing, for each data structure, the amount of space and time required for typical operations. For each algorithm, we examine the time required for key input types.
3. It will teach you how to measure the effectiveness of a data structure or algorithm. Only through such measurement can you determine which data structure in your toolkit is most appropriate for a new problem. The techniques presented also allow you to judge the merits of new data structures that you or others might invent.

ACTIVITY BASED LEARNING:

UNIT – II

Linked List with Yarn and Paper Bags

Learning Objectives:

4. Define, in their own words, a data structure
6. Define, in their own words, a linked list
8. Explain the steps to add a node to a linked list (front or back)
10. Explain the steps to delete a node from a linked list (front or back)
11. In this activity, students learn about the basic data structure linked list. Many students struggle to develop a mental picture of a linked list which increases the difficulty of them understanding the standard methods associated with this data structure (e.g., add to front of list, add to end of list, delete from front of list, delete from back of list, etc.). This activity is designed to provide that mental image for students and demonstrate the required steps for the essential methods needed to properly implement linked lists.

Name of the Topic

You Tube Link

DEQUEUE

https://www.youtube.com/watch?v= xC4m6O7VDJU

QUEUE

https://www.youtube.com/watch?v
=XuCbpw6Bj1U

LECTURE NOTES:

UNIT – II

LINEAR DATA STRUCTURES - LIST

What is a Data Structure?

A Data Structure is a collection of data elements which defines the way of storing and organizing data in a computer so that it can be used efficiently.

It comprises of

12. a collection of data elements
13. the relationships among them and
14. the functions or operations that can be applied to the data.
15.

Why is Data Structure needed?

16. It influences the ability of a computer to store/retrieve data to/from any location in the memory.
17. It enables a computer system to perform its task more efficiently.
18.

Classification of Data Structures

Data structures can be classified into two classes namely:

Primitive data structures and Non-Primitive data structures.

A primitive data structure refers to the fundamental data types which are supported by a programming language. Examples are integer, real, character, and boolean. Non-primitive data structures are created using primitive data structures.

Non-primitive data structures can further be classified into two categories:

Linear data structures and Non-linear data structures.

If the elements of a data structure are stored in a linear or sequential order, then it is a linear data structure. Examples are arrays, linked lists, stacks, and queues. Linear data structures can be implemented in memory in two different ways. One way is to use an array based implementation and the other is to use a linked list implementation.

If the elements of a data structure are not stored in a sequential order, then it is a non-linear data structure. Examples are trees and graphs.

ABSTRACT DATA TYPES (ADTs)

An abstract data type (ADT) is a set of operations. Abstract data types are mathematical abstractions. They do not mention how the set of operations is implemented.

An ADT is as an extension of modular design. Modularity has two advantages :

19. Debugging is easier
20. Many people can work on the modular program simultaneously. <u>Examples:</u>

21. Data structures such as lists, stacks, queues, trees and graphs along with their operations, can be viewed as abstract data types.

Fig: 1.2 An array of 6 elements represented in memory

Limitations of Arrays:

1. Arrays are of fixed size.
2. Contiguous memory locations may not be always available.
3. Insertion and deletion are quite difficult in an array as the elements are stored in consecutive memory locations and the shifting operation is costly.

23. To overcome the limitations of arrays, we use **linked lists.**

LIST ADT

A list is of the form a1,a2,a3,a4,...... ,an. The size of the list is n. The first element of the list

is a1 and an is the last element. The position of element ai in a list is i. A list of size 0 is called as a null list. Some of the operations that can be performed on a list are insert,

delete, find, print etc. Let us look at the operations with the help of an example. If the list contains the following elements 34,82,14,62,18,12 then

24. find(13) returns 3
25. insert(72,4) makes the list into 34,82,14,62,72,18,12 (i.e) 72 is inserted after position 4.
26. delete(18) makes the list into 34,82,14,62,72,12.
27. **Array Implementation of Lists** <u># assigning elements to list</u> list1 =[]

for i in range(0, 11):

list1.append(i)

accessing elements from a list for i in range(0, 11):

print(list1[i]) <u>Deletion from a list</u> list1 = [1, 2, 3, 4, 5]

print(list1)

deleting element del list1[2] print(list1)

Note : Arrays are generally not used to implement lists as the insertions and deletions is time consuming and expensive due to the shifting operation involved and the list size must also be known in advance.

LINKED LIST

28. The linked list consists of a series of nodes, which are not necessarily adjacent in
29. memory.
30. Each node contains two fields namely the data element and a pointer(called as the next pointer) to the next node as shown in Fig 1.3.
31.

32. he last node in the list

The next pointer of t points to NULL.

Data Next

element pointer

Fig Structure of a node in a linked list

Fig A Linked List

(Adapted from "Data Structures and Algorithm in Python")

In Fig 1.4, the linked list consists of 5 elements a1,a2,a3,a4,a5 respectively. Let us

assume that these 5 nodes reside in memory locations 890,496,345,900,254 respectively. Then we can represent our linked list as shown in Fig 1.5.

Fig : Linked List with actual pointer values

Linked List with a Header

A header is a special node that is used to keep track of a linked list. It is also called as a dummy node or sentinel node.

Fig 1.6 Linked List with a header

(Adapted from "Data Structures and Algorithm in Python")

Programming Details of a Linked List

Algorithm add_first(L, e):

newest = Node(e) {create new node instance storing reference to element e} newest.next = L.head {set new node's next to reference the old head node} L.head = newest {set variable head to reference the new node}

L.size = L.size + 1

g 1.7: Empty List with header

(Adapted from "Data Structures and Algorithm in Python")

Inserting an Element at the Tail of a Singly Linked List

We can also easily insert an element at the tail of the list, provided we keep a reference to the tail node, as shown in Figure. In this case, we create a new node, assign its next reference to None, set the next reference of the tail to point to this new node, and then update the tail reference itself to this new node

Algorithm add last(L, e):

newest = Node(e) {create new node instance storing reference to element e} newest.next = None {set new node's next to reference the None object}

L.tail.next = newest{make old tail node point to new node} L.tail = newest {set variable tail to reference the new node} L.size = L.size + 1 {increment the node count}

Insertion routine for linked lists

The following routine is used to insert an element x after a given position p.

```
insert( element_type x, LIST L, position p ):
{
position tmp_cell
tmp_cell = (position) malloc( sizeof (struct node) ) if( tmp_cell == NULL ):
fatal_error("Out of space!!!")
else
tmp_cell->element = x; tmp_cell->next = p->next; p->next = tmp_cell;
```

Fig 1.8: Insertion in a Linked List
(Adapted from "Data Structures and Algorithm Analysis in python")

Deletion routine for linked lists

Deletion Routine is used to delete a given element x from the list. It uses find_previous routine to locate the previous node of element x.

```
Algorithm remove first(L):
if L.head is None then
Indicate an error: the list is empty.
L.head = L.head.next {make head point to next node (or None)} L.size = L.size − 1 {decrement the node count}
```

Fig 1.9: Deletion from a Linked List
(Adapted from "Data Structures and Algorithm Analysis in C" by Mark Allen Weiss , 1997)

CIRCULARLY LINKED LIST

33. In circularly linked list the last node points to the first node/ header node of the linked list.
34. The last node of the list contains a pointer to the first node of the list.
35. The circular singly liked list has no beginning and no ending. There is no null value present in the next part of any of the nodes as shown in the Fig 1.10.
36. L

40
30
20
10

Fig 1.10: Circularly Linked ListAdvantages of Circular linked List

37. It allows to traverse the list starting at any point.
38. It allows quick access to the first and last records.
39. Circularly doubly linked list allows to traverse the list in either direction. Disadvantages of Circular linked List
40. Reversing a list is complex compared to linear linked list
41. If proper care is not taken in managing the pointers, it leads to infinite loop
42. Moving to previous node is difficult, as it is needed to complete an entire circle
43. **Declaration of node:**

class Node:

"""Lightweight, nonpublic class for storing a singly linked node.""" (omitted here; identical to that of LinkedStack. Node)

def init (self):

"""Create an empty queue."""

self. tail = None # will represent tail of queue self. size = 0 # number of queue elements

next

data

Fig 1.11: Structure of a node in a Circularly linked list Declaring a node with 2 fields.

1. data field
2. pointer to the next node as shown in the Fig 1.11

45. **Routine to create the list:**

- This routine creates a single node and get assigned to the tmpcell pointer.
- The next pointer of the last node in the list points to the first node or header node as shown in the Fig 1.12.

47. class CircularDoublyLinkedList: definit(self):

self.first = None

def get_node(self, index): current = self.first

for i in range(index): current = current.next if current == self.first:

return None return current

tmpcell

next

data

Fig 1.12: Node Creation in a Circularly linked list Routine to insert an element to the CLL

48. In Fig 1.13, inserts a given data in the already existing circular linked list.
49. P points to the Previous node to which the new node has to be inserted.
50. The new node is assigned to tmpcell.
51. **P**

tmpce ll
L
2
0
4
0
1
50
30
1
0
2

For example, if 50 should be inserted at the end position just by rearranging the pointers as numbered from 1 to 2 insertion can be done.

52. **Fig 1.13: Insertion in a Circularly linked list**

def insert_after(self, ref_node, new_node): new_node.prev = ref_node new_node.next = ref_node.next new_node.next.prev = new_node ref_node.next = new_node

def insert_before(self, ref_node, new_node): self.insert_after(ref_node.prev, new_node)

def insert_at_end(self, new_node): if self.first is None:

self.first = new_node new_node.next = new_node new_node.prev = new_node

else:

self.insert_after(self.first.prev, new_node) def insert_at_beg(self, new_node):

self.insert_at_end(new_node) self.first = new_node

Routine to delete an element from CLL

- In Fig 1.14, deletes a data from the given circular linked list.
- The Pointer P points to the node to be deleted.
- The Pointer T points to the previous node of the node to be deleted.
- For example, if 50 needs to be deleted just by rearranging the pointers as numbered 1 and 2 deletion can be done.

54. def remove(self, node):

if self.first.next == self.first: self.first = None

else:

node.prev.next = node.next node.next.prev = node.prev

if self.first == node: self.first = node.next

L
1
free ‘ P’ 2

4
0

3
0
2
0

1
0

5

0
P
T

Fig 1.14: Deletion from a Circularly linked list Routine to find an element

55. In Fig 1.15, finds a given element in the circular linked list.
56. P is a pointer which initially points to the first node in CLL and then moves down
57. the list to find the element.

def display(self):
if self.first is None: return
current = self.first while True:
print(current.data, end = ' ') current = current.next
P
L
40
30
20
10
if current == self.first: break

Fig 1.15: Find the element from a Circularly linked list Routine to print the elements from CLL

- In Fig 1.16, prints the element in the circular linked list.
- The list can be displayed in forward direction.
- P is a pointer which initially points to the first node in CLL and then moves

59. down the list to print the elements in the CLL using next field.

Fig 1.16: Print the element from a Circularly linked list

DOUBLY LINKED LIST

✓In Fig 1.17, a Linked list in which each node is linked to both its successor and its predecessor is said to be doubly linked list.

✓The ends of the list are defined by NULL pointers.

✓Each node in the list has two pointers, one to the next node and one to the previous one.

Fig 1.17: Doubly linked list

Advantages

·In doubly linked list, it is convenient to traverse lists backwards.

·It simplifies deletion, because no need to refer to a key by using a pointer to the previous cell. It is available in the node itself.

Disadvantages

·An extra field to the data structure, containing a pointer to the previous cell which adds to the space requirement and also doubles the cost of insertions and deletions because there are more pointers to fix.

Creating and performing various operations in a doubly linked list

class Node:

slots = _element , _prev , _next # streamline memory def init (self, element, prev, next): # initialize node's fields

self. element = element # user's element

self. prev = prev # previous node reference

self. next = next # next node reference

Declaring a node with 3 fields.

60. data field
61. pointer to next node
62. pointer to previous node
63.

Routine to create the DLL

64. This routine creates a single node and get assigned to the tmpcell pointer. The next field and prev field are assigned NULL as shown in the Fig 1.18.
65. **Fig 1.18: Node Creation in Doubly linked list**

def init (self):

"""Create an empty list."""

self. header = self. Node(None, None, None) self. trailer = self. Node(None, None, None)

self. header. next = self. trailer # trailer is after header self. trailer. prev = self. header # header is before trailer self. size = 0 # number of elements

Routine to insert an element to the DLL

66. In Fig 1.19,inserts a given data in the already existing doubly linked list.
67. P points to the Previous node to which the new node has to be inserted.
68. The new node is assigned to tmpcell.
69. For example if 25 should be inserted between 20 and 30 just by rearranging the pointers as numbered from 1 to 4 insertion can be done.
70. def insert between(self, e, predecessor, successor):
    """Add element e between two existing nodes and return new node.""" newest = self. Node(e, predecessor, successor) # linked to neighbors predecessor. next = newest
    successor. prev = newest self. size += 1
    return newest
    Routine to delete an element from DLL
71. In Fig 1.20, deletes a data from the given doubly linked list.
72. The Pointer P points to the node to be deleted.
73. The Pointer T points to the previous node of the node to be deleted.
74. For example if 20 needs to be deleted just by rearranging the pointers as numbered deletion can be done.
75. 40
    30
    20
    10
    L

T P

Fig 1.20: Deletion from a Doubly linked list

def delete node(self, node):
"""Delete nonsentinel node from the list and return its element.""" predecessor = node. prev
successor = node. next predecessor. next = successor successor. prev = predecessor self. size −= 1
element = node. element # record deleted element
node. prev = node. next = node. element = None # deprecate node return element # return deleted element

Routine to find an element

76. This routine finds a given element in the doubly linked list.
77. P is a pointer which initially points to the first node in DLL and then moves down the list to find the element.
78. def len (self):
    """Return the number of elements in the list.""" return self. size
    def is empty(self):
    """Return True if list is empty.""" return self. size == 0

Routine to print the elements from DLL

79. This routine prints the element in the doubly linked list.
80. The list can be displayed both in forward and reverse direction.
81. P is a pointer which initially points to the first node in DLL and then moves down the list to print the elements in the DLL using next field.
82. The list can be printed in backward direction by using the prev field.
83.

```
def display(self):
if self.first is None: return
current = self.first while True:
print(current.data, end = ' ') current = current.next
if current == self.first: break
```

LINKED LIST APPLICATIONS

Few applications of List are:

84/85. Polynomial ADT (Simple way to represent single-variable polynomial)
86/87. 2. Radix sort
88/89. 3. Multilist
90. 1. The Polynomial ADT:
91. Some other applications of the linked list are:

Images are linked with each other. So, an image viewer software uses a linked list to view the previous and the next images using the previous and next buttons.

Web pages can be accessed using the previous and the next URL links which are linked using linked list.

The music players also use the same technique to switch between music.

To keep the track of turns in a multi player game, a circular linked listis used.

STACK ADTs

- A stack is an abstract data type (ADT) such that an instance S supports the following two methods:

93. ◦ S.push(e): Add element e to the top of stack S.

- S.pop( ): Remove and return the top element from the stack S; an error occurs if the stack is empty

95. ◦ The following accessor methods for convenience:

- S.top( ): Return a reference to the top element of stack S, without removing it; an error occurs if the stack is empty.

97. ◦ S.is empty( ): Return True if stack S does not contain any elements.

◦

99.): Return the number of elements in stack S; in Pyt
ith the special method len .
len(S hon, implemented

this w

Simple Array-Based Stack Implementation

A stack quite easily by storing its elements in a Python list. The list class already supports adding an element to the end with the append method, and removing the last element with the pop method, so it is natural to align the top of the stack at the end of the list,

Implementing a stack with a Python list, storing the top element in the rightmost cell.

Realization of a stack S as an adaptation of a Python list L.

Stack Method

Realization with Python list

S.push(e)

L.append(e)

S.pop( )

L.pop( )

S.top( )

L[−1]S.is empty( ) len(L)=0

len(S)

len()

Definition for an Empty Exception

```
class Empty(Exception):
"""Error attempting to access an element from an empty container."""
pass
```

Implementing a stack using a Python list as storage.

```
class ArrayStack:
"""LIFO Stack implementation using a Python list as underlying storage."""
def init (self): """Create an empty stack."""
self. data = [ ] # nonpublic list instance
def len (self): """Return the number of elements in the stack"""
return len(self. data)
def is_empty(self): """Return True if the stack is empty."""
return len(self. data) == 0
```

def push(self, e): """*Add element e to the top of the stack.*"""

self. data.append(e) # *new item stored at end of list*

def top(self): """*Return (but do not remove) the element at the top of the stack.*

Raise Empty exception if the stack is empty. """

if self.is_empty( ):

raise Empty(Stack is empty)

return self. data[−1] # *the last item in the list*

def pop(self): """*Remove and return the element from the top of the stack (i.e., LIFO). Raise Empty exception if the stack is empty.* """

if self.is empty( ):

raise Empty(Stack is empty)

return self. data.pop( ) # *remove last item from list*

Queue Data Structure

Another fundamental data structure is the queue. It is a close "cousin" of the stack, as a queue is a collection of objects that are inserted and removed according to the first-in, first-out (FIFO) principle.

A metaphor for this terminology is a line of people waiting to get on an amusement park ride. People waiting for such a ride enter at the back of the line and get on the ride from the front of the line.

Queue ADTs

Queue abstract data type defines a collection that keeps objects in a sequence, where element access and deletion are restricted to the first element in the queue, and element insertion is restricted to the back of the sequence.

100. The queue abstract data type (ADT) - two fundamental methods for a queue Q:
101. Q.enqueue(e): *Add element e to the back of queue Q.*
102. Q.dequeue( ): *Remove and return the first element from queue Q; an error occurs if the queue is empty.*
103. The queue ADT - supporting methods
104. Q.first( ): *Return a reference to the element at the front of queue Q, without removing it; an error occurs if the queue is empty.*
105. Q.is empty( ):*Return True if queue Q does not contain any elements.*

107.

len(Q):*Return the number ofel3e5ments in queue Q;*[1]

108. Array-Based Queue Implementation

An enqueue element e is done by calling append(e) , which adds an element to the end of the list. pop(0), as opposed to pop( ), is done to intentionally remove the first element from the list when dequeuing.

class ArrayQueue:

"""FIFO queue implementation using a Python list as underlying storage."""

DEFAULT CAPACITY = 10 # moderate capacity for all new queues def init (self): """Create an empty queue."""

self. data = [None]*ArrayQueue.DEFAULT CAPACITY self. size = 0 self. front = 0

def len (self):"""Return the number of elements in the queue.""" return self. size

def is empty(self): """Return True if the queue is empty.""" return self. size == 0

def first(self):""Return (but do not remove) the element at the front of the queue. Raise Empty exception if the queue is empty."""

if self.is empty( ):

raise Empty(Queue is empty) return self. data[self. front]

def dequeue(self): """Remove and return the first element of the queue (i.e., FIFO). Raise Empty exception if the queue is empty. """

if self.is empty( ):

raise Empty(Queue is empty) answer = self. data[self. front]

self. data[self. front] = None # help garbage collection self. front = (self. front + 1) % len(self. data)

self. size −= 1 return answer

def enqueue(self, e):

"""Add an element to the back of queue.""" if self. size == len(self. data):

self. resize(2 len (self.data)) # double the array size avail = (self. front + self. size) % len(self. data) self. data[avail] = e

self. size += 1

def resize(self, cap): # we assume cap >= len (self) """Resize to a new list of capacity >= len(self)."""

old = self. data # keep track of existing list

self. data = [None] * cap # allocate list with new capacity walk = self. front

for k in range(self. size): # only consider existing elements self. data[k] = old[walk] # intentionally shift indices walk = (1 + walk) % len(old) # use old size as modulus self. front = 0

Double-Ended Queues

A queue-like data structure that supports insertion and deletion at both the front and the back of the queue is called a double ended queue, or deque, which is usually pronounced “deck” to avoid confusion with the dequeue method of the regular queue ADT, which is pronounced like the abbreviation "D.Q."

The Deque Abstract Data Type

Deque D supports the following methods:
D.add first(e): Add element e to the front of deque D. D.add last(e): Add element e to the back of deque D.
D.delete first( ): Remove and return the first element from deque D; an error occurs if the deque is empty.
D.delete last( ): Remove and return the last element from deque D; an error occurs if the deque is empty.
Additionally, the deque ADT will include the following accessors:
D.first( ): Return (but do not remove) the first element of deque D; an error occurs if the deque is empty.
D.last( ): Return (but do not remove) the last element of deque D; an error occurs if the deque is empty.
D.is_empty( ): Return True if deque D does not contain any elements.
len(D): Return the number of elements in deque D; in Python, implemented this with the special method len .
mplementing a Deque with a Circular Array

class ArrayDeQueue:
"""*FIFO queue implementation using a Python list as underlying storage.*"""
DEFAULT CAPACITY = 10 # moderate capacity for all new queues def init (self): """Create an empty queue."""
self. data = [None]*ArrayQueue.DEFAULT CAPACITY self. size = 0 self. front = 0
def len (self):"""Return the number of elements in the queue.""" return self. size
def is_empty(self): """Return True if the queue is empty.""" return self.size == 0
def first(self):""Return (but do not remove) the element at the front of the queue. Raise Empty exception if the queue is empty."""

if self.is_empty( ):

raise Empty(Queue is empty) return self. data[self. front]

def del_first(self): """Remove and return the first element of the queue (i.e., FIFO). Raise Empty exception if the queue is empty. """

if self.is_empty( ):

raise Empty(Queue is empty) answer = self. data[self. front]

self. data[self. front] = None # help garbage collection self. front = (self. front + 1) % len(self. data)

self. size −= 1 return answer

def add_last(self, e):

"""Add an element to the back of queue.""" if self. size == len(self. data):

self. resize(2*len (self.data)) # double the array size avail = (self. front + self. size) % len(self. data)

self. data[avail] = e self. size += 1

def last()

back = (self. front + self. size − 1) % len(self. data) return self.data[self.back]

Deques in the Python Collections Module

class collections.deque(list) from collections import deque

The library deque constructor also supports an optional maxlen parameter to force a fixed-length deque. However, if a call to append at either end is invoked when the deque is full, it does not throw an error; instead, it causes one element to be dropped from the opposite side. That is, calling appendleft when the deque is full causes an implicit pop from the right side to make room for the new element.

PART A QUESTIONS WITH ANSWERS

What is Stack?

A stack is a list with the restriction that inserts and deletes can be performed in only one position, namely the end of the list called the top.

List the operations performed on stack.

PUSH – This operation is used to insert an element on to the stack. POP – This operation is used to delete the most recently inserted element

What is the use top pointer?

It is used to indicate the top of the stack element. Used to check whether stack isempty(if top==1) delete the most recently inserted element.

List the applications of stack.

110. Balancing Paranthesis
111. Conversion of Infix Expression to Postfix Expression 3.Evaluation of Postfix Expression
112. Function Call
113. Convert the infix expression x^y/(5*z)+2 to postfix form.

The Postfix form is: xy^5z*/2+

What do you mean by Balancing Paranthesis?

An algebraic expression is valid if for every open bracket there is a corresponding closing bracket. Example:{(a + b) * [(c + d)/e] }

How to check the overflow condition in stack?

If the top pointer reaches the maximum size of the stack then physically and logically the stack is full

Why stack is called LIFO list?

The last element inserted into the stack is the first element to be deleted. For this reason, stack is called Last-In First-Out list.

What are the limitations in the stack

when array used as home of stack? The Array is finite collection of elements and in stack the number of elements is unlimited. As the stack dynamically changes the attempts to insert more elements than the array size cause overflow

Define Queue ADT

A queue is an ordered collection of items where insertion is done at a end called the rear and deletion is done at the other end called front. The technique or discipline followed by queue is FIFO(First In First Out). The first element inserted in the queue will be the first element to be deleted.

What are the operations performed on Queue?

The primitive operations of queue are enqueue and dequeue. enqueue: inserts an element at the end of the list called rear end. dequeue: deletes thc element at the start of the list called the front end

What is double ended queue?

In deque insertion and deletion operations are performed at both ends of the Queue. Deque can bi implemented using circular array.

List down the applications of deque.

•Palindrome checker

•Job scheduling algorithm for multiple processors.

•Undo redo operations in software applications.

What is List ADT?

Abstract Data type (ADT) is a type (or class) for objects whose behaviour is defined by a set of value and a set of operations. The definition of ADT only mentions what operations are to be performed but not how these operations will be implemented. ... Now we'll define three ADTs namely List ADT, Stack ADT, Queue ADT

Define Linked list?

A linked list is a sequence of data elements, which are connected together via links. Each data element contains a connection to another data element in form of a pointer. Python does not have linked lists in its standard library.

Define Singly link list?

A linked list is a sequence of data elements, which are connected together via links. Each data element contains a connection to another data element in form of a pointer. Python does not have linked lists in its standard library.

Define Doubly Link List?

A Doubly Linked List (DLL) contains an extra pointer, typically called *previous pointer*, together with next pointer and data which are there in singly linked list

Define circular Link list?

The circular linked list is a kind of linked list. First thing first, the node is an element of the list, and it has two parts that are, data and next. Data represents the data stored in the node, and next is the pointer that will point to the next node. Head will point to the first element of the list, and tail will point to the last element in the list. In the simple linked list, all the nodes will point to their next element and tail will point to null.

PART B QUESTIONS

115. Explain in detail about stack and implement the same using array.
116. Explain in detail about stack and implement the same using linked list.
118. Discuss the various applications of stack with examples.
120. Write an algorithm to create two stacks using single array
123. Explain in detail the array based implementation of Queue ADT.
125. Explain in detail the linked list implementation of Queue ADT.
126. What is a circular queue? Write the procedure to insert an element to circular queue and delete an element from a circular queue using array implementation?
128. Write functions to insert, deletemin and display a node from a priority queue.
130. Illustrate with a neat example the implementation of a double ended queue.
132. Explain in Detail about Singly Link list with example Program?
134. Explain in Detail about Doubly Link list with example Program?
136. Explain in Detail about Circular Link list with example Program?
138. Explain in Detail about Linked list with example Program?
139. Explain in Detail about Array list Implementation with example Program?
140.

SUPPORTIVE ONLINE CERTIFICATION COURSES

COURSERA

Data Structures

Data Structures and Algorithms Python Data Structures

UDEMY

Data Structures and Algorithms: In-Depth using Python Python Data Structures A to Z

NPTEL

Programming , Data Structures and Algorithm Using Python

REAL TIME APPLICATIONS

INDUSTRY

Text editor

Your regular text editor has the functionality of editing and storing text while it is being written or edited. So, there are multiple changes in the cursor position. To achieve high efficiency, we require a fast data structure for insertion and modification. And the ordinary character arrays take time for storing strings.

You can experiment with other data structures like gap buffers and ropes to solve these issues. Your end objective will be to attain faster concatenation than the usual strings by occupying smaller contiguous memory space.

141. Converting infix to postfix expressions.
142. Undo operation is also carried out through **stacks**.
143. Syntaxes in languages are parsed using **stacks**.
144. It is used in many virtual machines like JVM.
145. Forward – backward surfing in browser.
146. History of visited websites.
147. **Content Beyond Syllabus**

Backtracking using Stack

Backtracking is an algorithmic-technique for solving problems recursively by trying to build a solution incrementally, one piece at a time, removing those solutions that fail to satisfy the constraints of the problem at any point of time (by time, here, is referred to the time elapsed till reaching any level of the search tree).

For example, consider the SudoKo solving Problem, we try filling digits one by one. Whenever we find that current digit cannot lead to a solution, we remove it (backtrack) and try next digit. This is better than naive approach (generating all possible combinations of digits and then trying every combination one by one) as it drops a set of permutations whenever it backtracks.

Example: Rat in a Maze

A Maze is given as N*N binary matrix of blocks where source block is the upper left most block i.e., maze[0][0] and destination block is lower rightmost block i.e., maze[N-1][N-1]. A rat starts from source and has to reach the destination.

The rat can move only in two directions: forward and down In the maze matrix, 0 means the block is a dead end and 1 means the block can be used in the path from source to destination. Note that this is a simple version of the typical Maze problem. For example, a more complex version can be that the rat can move in 4 directions and a more complex version can be with a limited number of moves.

Initial Maze

Final Maze

Approach: Form a recursive function, which will follow a path and check if the path reaches the destination or not. If the path does not reach the destination then backtrack and try other paths.

Algorithm:

148. Create a solution matrix, initially filled with 0's.
150. Create a recursive function, which takes initial matrix, output matrix and position of rat (i, j).
152. if the position is out of the matrix or the position is not valid then return.
153. Mark the position output[i][j] as 1 and check if the current position is destination or not. If destination is reached print the output matrix and return.
154. Recursively call for position (i+1, j) and (i, j+1).
156. Unmark position (i, j), i.e output[i][j] = 0.
157.

Online References

https://www.geeksforgeeks.org/rat-in-a-maze-backtracking-2/https://www.youtube.com/watch?v=xy0pIcoWCd0

TEXT & REFERENCE BOOKS

Text Books

158. Michael T. Goodrich, Roberto Tamassia, and Michael H. Goldwasser, "Data Structures & Algorithms in Python", John Wiley & Sons Inc., 2013
159. Lee, Kent D., Hubbard, Steve, "Data Structures and Algorithms with Python" Springer Edition 2015
160. Reference Books

1. Rance D. Necaise, "Data Structures and Algorithms Using Python", John Wiley & Sons, 2011
2. Aho, Hopcroft, and Ullman, "Data Structures and Algorithms", Pearson Education, 1983.
3. Thomas H. Cormen, Charles E. Leiserson, Ronald L. Rivest, and Clifford Stein, "Introduction to Algorithms", Second Edition, McGraw Hill, 2002.
4. Mark Allen Weiss, "Data Structures and Algorithm Analysis in C++", Fourth Edition, Pearson Education, 2014

162. Additional Reference Books

1. Data Structures and Algorithms Made Easy: Data Structures and Algorithmic Puzzles by Narasimha Karumanchi , Careermonk Publications, 5th edition, 2017

MINI PROJECT

163. Implement a program that can input an expression in postfix notation and output its value.
164. When a share of common stock of some company is sold, the capital gain (or, sometimes, loss) is the difference between the share's selling price and the price originally paid to buy it. This rule is easy to understand for a single share, but if we sell multiple shares of stock bought over a long period of time, then we must identify the shares

actually being sold. A standard accounting principle for identifying which shares of a stock were sold in such a case is to use a FIFO protocol—the shares sold are the ones that have been held the longest (indeed, this is the default method built into several personal finance software packages). For example, suppose we buy 100 shares at $20 each on day 1, 20 shares at $24 on day 2, 200 shares at $36 on day 3, and then sell 150 shares on day 4 at $30 each. Then applying the FIFO protocol means that of the 150 shares sold, 100 were bought on day 1, 20 were bought on day 2, and 30 were bought on day 3. The capital gain in this case would therefore be 100 · 10+20 · 6+30 ·(−6), or $940. Write a program that takes as input a sequence of transactions of the form "buy x share(s) at y each" or "sell x share(s) at y each," assuming that the transactions occur on consecutive days and the values x and y are integers. Given this input sequence, the output should be the total capital gain (or loss) for the entire sequence, using the FIFO protocol to identify shares.

165. Design an ADT for a two-color, double-stack ADT that consists of two stacks—one "red" and one "blue"—and has as its operations color-coded versions of the regular stack ADT operations. For example, this ADT should support both a red push operation and a blue push operation. Give an efficient implementation of this ADT using a single array whose capacity is set at some value N that is assumed to always be larger than the sizes of the red and blue stacks combined.

166.

LECTURE NOTES: UNIT – IV

NON-LINEAR DATA STRUCTURES – TREES

167. Non-Linear Data Structures

168. The data structure where data items are not organized sequentially is called non linear data structure. Trees and Graphs are the examples of Non-linear data structures.

169. Tree

170. **Figure Tree data structure**

A tree can be used to represent any general hierarchical information as shown in below figure

Figure-Generic Tree

A Tree is a Non-linear Data Structure, in which the elements are represented as nodes and the nodes are connected with each other by means of edges as shown in below figure. The starting node of the tree is called as the root node. A tree imposes a hierarchical structure on a collection of elements. Trees are used for wide variety of applications like organization of information in database systems, syntactic structure of programs in compiler, electrical circuits, and representation of mathematical formulas.

3. Basic Terminologies used in Trees

172. **Root:** The first node from where the tree originates is called as a root node. In any tree, there must be only one root node. We can never have multiple root nodes in a tree data structure.

Edge: The connecting link between any two nodes is called as an edge. In a tree with n number of nodes, there are exactly (n-1) number of edges.

Parent: The node which has a branch from it to any other node is called as a parent node. In other words, the node which has one or more children is called as a parent node. In a tree, a parent node can have any number of child nodes **Child:** The node which is a descendant of some node is called as a child node.

All the nodes except root node are child nodes.

Siblings: Nodes which belong to the same parent are called as siblings.

In other words, nodes with the same parent are sibling nodes.

Degree: Degree of a node is the total number of children of that node.

Degree of a tree is the highest degree of a node among all the nodes in the tree.

Internal Node: The node which has at least one child is called as an internal node. Internal nodes are also called as non-terminal nodes. Every non-leaf node is an internal node. A sample tree is given in figure

Sample Tree

Leaf Node: The node which does not have any child is called as a leaf node. Leaf nodes are also called as external nodes or terminal nodes.

Level: In a tree, each step from top to bottom is called as level of a tree. The level count starts with 0 and increments by 1 at each level or step.

Height: Total number of edges that lies on the longest path from a particular node to any leaf node is called as **height of that node. Height of a tree** is the height of root node. Height of all leaf nodes = 0. The height of the sample tree

shown in figure is 3.

Depth: Total number of edges from root node to a particular node is called as **depth of that node. Depth of a tree** is the total number of edges from root node to a leaf node in the longest path. Depth of the root node = 0.The terms

"level" and "depth" are used interchangeably.

Subtree: In a tree, each child from a node forms a subtree recursively. Every child node forms a subtree on its parent node

Forest: A forest is a disjoint union of trees. A set of disjoint trees (or forests) is

obtained by deleting the root and the edges connecting the root node to nodes at level 1. For example, the below Figure shows a forest

Figure Forest

Types of Trees

There are different types of trees like

173. Binary tree,
174. Binary search tree,
175. AVL tree and
176. M-way search tree
177. Binary Tree

A Tree is said be a binary tree if each node in the tree has at most two children i.e either 0 or 1 or 2 children. So each node in a binary tree has 0 child or 1 child or 2 children as shown in below figure 3.5.

Figure 3.5: Binary Tree

Binary Tree Representation

A binary tree can be represented in the following two ways

178. Array Representation/ Static Representation
180. Linked list Representation/ Dynamic Representation

181. **Array Representation/ Static Representation:** A single dimensional array can be used to represent a binary tree. The nodes in the tree are stored recursively as parent, left child and right child as shown in below figure 3.6. In case if a child does not exist that location is left as empty
182. Figure 3.6 Array representation of Binary tree Logic to find the location of parent, left child and right child
183. If index of Root=i
184. Index of Left child= 2i+1
185. Index of Right Child=2i+2
186. of the above binary tree is

Example: Consider the below binary tree

The array representation

The main drawback of array representation of binary tree is lot of memory space gets wasted.

187. Linked list Representation/ Dynamic Representation
188. Double linked list used to represent a binary tree. In a double linked list, every node consists of three fields. First field for storing left child address, second for storing actual data and third for storing right child address. In this linked list representation, a node has the following structure

node

lchild stores the address of left child and rchild stores the address of right child. Types of Binary Trees

Example: Consider the below binary tree

The linked list representation of the above binary tree is given in figure 3.7

Figure 3.7: Linked list representation of Binary tree

1. Operations on Binary Tree

1. **Insertion:**Insertion of the elements is done at the leaf nodes. Always a node is inserted as leaf node, whether to make the new node as left child or right child is
2. decided based on user input.
3. **Deletion:**In deletion a leaf node in the tree is deleted after searching for the node, once node is identified its disconnected from its parents by changing its
4. parent left link or right link as null.
5. **Traversal:**Visiting every node in the tree only once is called traversal there are four different types of traversals namely In-order traversal, Pre-order traversal,
6. Post-order traversal and Level-order traversal.
7. In-order Traersal
8. In this traversal method, the left subtree is visited first, then the root and later the right sub-tree. The in-order traversal algorithm uses the below three steps recursively

   Algorithm

   1. Traverse the left-subtree
   2. Visit the node
   3. Traverse the right-subtree.

10. **Recursive Function**

    Algorithm

    inorder(p):

    if p has a left child lc then

    inorder(lc) {recursively traverse the left subtree of p} perform the "visit" action for position p

    if p has a right child rc then

    inorder(rc) {recursively traverse the right subtree of p}

    Example: Consider the below binary tree,

In-order

Traversal:

11. Pre-order Traersal
12. Preorder traversal will create a copy of the tree. Preorder Traversal is also used to get the prefix expression of an expression. The pre-order traversal algorithm uses

    the below three steps recursively

    Algorithm
13. Visit the node
14. Traverse the left-subtree
15. Traverse the right-subtree.
16. **Recursive Function**

```
def preorder(self):
"""Generate a preorder iteration of positions in the tree.""" if not self.isempty( ):
for p in self.Subtree_preorder(self.root( )):# start recursion yield p
def subtree preorder(self, p):
"""Generate a preorder iteration of positions in subtree rooted at p.""" yield p # visit p before its subtrees
for c in self.children(p): # for each child c
for other in self.subtree_preorder(c): # do preorder of c's subtree yield other # yielding each to our caller
```

Example: Consider the below binary tree,

Pre –order Traversal

Pre-order Traversal

17. Post-order Traersal
18. In this traversal method, the left subtree is traversed first, then right subtree and later visit the node. The post-order traversal algorithm uses the below three steps
    recursively
    Algorithm
19. Traverse the left-subtree
20. Traverse the right-subtree.
21. Visit the node
22. **Recursive Function**

```
def postorder(self):
"""Generate a postorder iteration of positions in the tree.""" if not self.isempty( ):
for p in self.Subtree_postorder(self.root( )):# start recursion
yield p
def subtree postorder(self, p):
"""Generate a postorder iteration of positions in subtree rooted at p.""" for c in self.children(p): # for each child c
for other in self.subtree_postorder(c): # do postorder of c's subtree yield other # yielding each to our caller
yield p
```

Example: Consider the below binary tree

23. Leel-order Traersal
24. In this traversal method, all nodes present at one level are printed first then the next level. The following two steps are recursively implemented

    Algorithm
25. Visit all the nodes from left to right in a level
26. Move to the next level.
27. Repeat step 1 to 2 until all the levels are completed
28. **Recursive Function**

    /*Function to print level order traversal of tree*/ printLevelorder(tree)
    for d = 1 to height(tree) printCurrentLevel(tree, d)
    /*Function to print all nodes at a current level*/ printCurrentLevel(tree, level)
    if tree is NULL then return
    if level is 1, then print(tree->data)
    else if level greater than 1, then printCurrentLevel(tree->left, level-1) printCurrentLevel(tree->right, level-1)
    Example: Consider the below binary tree

2. Constructing a Binary Tree from Traversal Results

30. We can construct a binary tree if we are given at least two traversal results. The first traversal must be the in-order traversal and the second can be either pre-
order or post-order traversal.

The in-order traversal result will be used to determine the left and the right child nodes, and the pre-order/ post-order can be used to determine the root node.

For **example**, consider the traversal results given below:

In–order Traversal: **D B E A F C G**

Pre–order Traversal: **A B D E C F G**

Here, we have the in-order traversal sequence and pre-order traversal sequence. Follow the steps given below to construct the tree:

Step 1 : Use the pre-order sequence to determine the root node of the tree. The first element would be the root node.

Step 2: Elements on the left side of the root node in the in-order traversal sequence form the left sub-tree of the root node. Similarly, elements on the right side of the root node in the in-order traversal sequence form the right sub-tree of the root node.

Step 3: Recursively select each element from pre-order traversal sequence and create its left and right sub-trees from the in-order traversal sequence.

31. Look at the below Figure which constructs the tree from it traversal results.

32.

For Example, consider the below in-order and post-order traversals

In–order Traversal: **D B H E I A F J C G**

Post order Traversal: **D H I E B J F G C A**

Binary Tree
Traversal
https://www.youtube.com/watch?v=L88rWs3xpyU
Animation
Binary Tree Traversal
http://www.cs.armstrong.edu/liang/animation/web/BST.html
Types of Binary Trees

33. **Full Binary Tree:** A full binary tree (sometimes proper binary tree or 2-tree) is a tree in which every node other than the leaves has two children. Its also known as a perfect binary tree.
5. **Complete Binary Tree:** A complete binary tree is a binary tree in which every
6. level, except possibly the last, is possible.

completely filled, and all nodes are as far left as

Fig Full Binary Tree Fig Complete Binary Tree

7. Skewed Binary Tree:
8. A skewed binary tree is a type of binary tree in which all the nodes have only either one child or no child. These are two types

Left Skewed Binary Tree: These are those skewed binary trees in which all the nodes are having a left child or no child at all. It is a left side dominated tree. All the right children remain as null.

Right Skewed Binary Tree: These are those skewed binary trees in which all the nodes are having a right child or no child at all. It is a right side dominated tree. All

the left children remain as null.

9. Expression Tree

10.

Expression tree is a binary tree in which each internal node corresponds to operator and each leaf node corresponds to operand. For example the expression tree for the expression (a+b) *(c-d) is shown in figure 3.8

Figure 3.8: Expression Tree

Construction of an Expression Tree from post fix expression

For constructing expression tree we use a stack. We loop through input expression and do following for every character.

11. Read one symbol at a time from the postfix expression.
12. Check if the symbol is an operand or operator.
13. If the symbol is an operand, create a one node tree and pushed a pointer onto a stack
14. If the symbol is an operator, pop two pointer from the stack namely T1 & T2 and form a new tree with root as the operator, T1 & T2 as a left and right child
15. A pointer to this new tree is pushed onto the stack
16. **Example:** construct an expression tree for the post fix expression a b +c *

The first two symbols are operands, we create one-node tree and push a pointer to them onto the stack.

Next, read a'+' symbol, so two pointers to tree are popped, a new tree is formed and push a pointer to it onto the stack.

Next, **'c'** is read, we create one node tree and push a pointer to it onto the stack.

Finally, the last symbol is read ' * ', we pop two tree pointers and form a new tree with a, ' * ' as root, and a pointer to the final tree remains on the stack.

<u>Construction of an Expression Tree from infix expression</u>

There are two methods to draw the expression tree for infix expression

<u>Method-1:</u>Convert the given expression into a post fix expression and draw the expression tree.

<u>Method-2:</u>We can draw the expression tree directly from the infix expression by using the operator precedence and associativity. The precedence and associativity of the operators is shown in the below table 3.1

Operator	**Priority**	**Associativity**
^	5	

Right to left

*, /

4

Left to right

+, -

3

Left to right

Table 3.1 : Operator Precedence

Algorithm:

17. Identify the least priority operator in the infix expression, if two operators are having equal priority use associativity to identify the least priority one.
18. Construct the tree with the least priority operator with LHS expression as left subtree and RHS as right subtree.
19. Repeat step 1 to 2 until all the operators are scanned.
20. Example: Construct a binary tree for the expression (a+b*c) +((d*e+f)*g)

Step-1: The least precedence operator from the expression is +

Step-2: The least precedence operator from the left subtree is + and from right subtree is * .

Step-3: After processing next level the tree is as shown below

The final expression tree is

Few Points to note about Expression Tree

21. Constants and variables are always leaves of the tree.

22. Operators are inner nodes, and they have as many children as the operator takes: unary minus has one child, binary operators have 2.
23. The tree structure encodes the order of operations: the closer something is to the bottom of the tree, the higher its precedence. The root of the tree is the operator that should be performed last.
24.

25. Threaded Binary Tree
26. In-order traversal of a Binary tree can either be done using recursion or with the use of a auxiliary stack. The idea of threaded binary trees is to make in-order traversal faster and do it without stack and without recursion.

    A binary tree is made threaded by making all right child pointers that would normally be NULL point to the in-order successor of the node (if it exists).

    Types of Threaded binary trees

    There are two types of threaded binary trees.
27. **Single Threaded:** Where a NULL right pointer is made to point to the in-order successor (if successor exists)
5. **Double Threaded:** Where both left and right NULL pointers are made to point to in-order predecessor and in-order successor respectively. The predecessor threads
6. Figure Threaded Binary Tree

    are useful for reverse in-order traversal and post-order traversal.

    The threads are also useful for fast accessing ancestors of a node. The above figure

    shows an example Single Threaded Binary Tree and Double Threaded binary tree. The dotted lines represent threads.

In-order Traversal using Threaded Binary Tree

Rest of the nodes in the threaded binary tree are traversed similarly

2. Binary Search Trees

8. A binary search tree is a special kind of binary tree where nodes are arranged in specific order satisfying the below property.

    In a binary search tree (BST), each node contains-
9. Only **smaller values** in its **left sub tree**
10. Only **larger values** in its **right sub tree**
11. Figure 3.10: Binary Search Tree

    The operation like insertion, deletion and searching are simplified in a binary search tree compared to a binary tree. A sample BST is given in figure 3.10.
12. Operations on BST
13. **The following operations can be performed on a binary search Tree**

v. Searching
v. Insertion
v. Deletion
v. Traversal
v. Find Min
v. Find Max

15. Searching
16. The algorithm depends on the property of BST that if each left subtree has values below root and each right subtree has values above the root.
    Algorithm: search(root)
17. If root == NULL
18. return NULL;
19. If number == root->data
20. return root->data;
21. If number < root->data
22. return search(root->left)
23. If number > root->data
24. return search(root->right)
25. Insertion
26. Inserting a value in the correct position is similar to searching because we try to maintain the rule that the left subtree is lesser than root and the right subtree is larger than root.
    Steps to insert
27. Start searching from the root node,
28. if the data is less than the key value, search for the empty location in the left subtree and insert the data.
29. Otherwise, search for the empty location in the right subtree and insert the data.
30. Algorithm: insert(root, data)

    1. If node == NULL
    2. return createNode(data)
    3. if (data < node->data)

32. 4.node->left = insert(node->left, data); 5.else if (data > node->data)
    6. node->right = insert(node->right, data); 7.return node;
    Example: Construct a Binary search tree with the elements 43, 10, 79, 90, 12, 54, 11,9,50
    The construction of BST is a sequence of insertion operation starting from an empty BST

33. Deletion Operation
34. Deletion in a binary search tree involves three cases **Case-1:**Deleting a node with no child (leaf node) **Case-2:**Deleting a node having one children

    Case-3: Deleting a node having two children

Case-1: Deleting a node with no child (leaf node)

The node to be deleted is a leaf node , we just find the node and disconnect it from the parent node.

Example: Delete 50 from the below BST

Before Deletion After Deletion

Case-2: Deleting a node having one child

In the second case, the node to be deleted lies has a single child node. In such a case the following steps are used:

35. Replace that node with its child node.
36. Remove the child node from its original position.
37.

Example: Delete 54 from the below BST

Before Deletion After Deletion

Case-2: Deleting a node having two children

In the third case, the node to be deleted has two children. In such a case follow the steps below:

38. Get the in-order successor/ Predecessor of that node.
39. Replace the node with the in-order successor/ Predecessor. 3.Remove the in-order successor/ Predecessor from its original position. In-order Successor (n) = Smallest element in the right subtree
40. In-order Predecessor(n) = Largest element in the left subtree.

Example: Consider deleting the node 43 from the below BST

Step-1: Getting the in-order Successor of 43. From the given BST, the in-order successor(43)= 90.

Step-2: We replace 43 with 50

Step-3: Deleting the in-order successor node

After deleting 43

41. Traersal:
42. Binary Search Tree traversal is same as binary tree traversal
43. Find Minimum and Maximum
44. Finding the minimum and maximum is very simple in binary search tree. A complete left subtree traversal until left subtree is null gives the minimum element and a complete right subtree traversal until its null gives the

maximum element.

Algorithm: find_Max(root)

1. Traverse the node from root to right recursively until right is NULL.
2. The node whose right is NULL is the node with maximum value.

46. Algorithm: find_Min (root)
47. Traverse the node from root to left recursively until right is NULL.
48. The node whose left is NULL is the node with minimum value.
49. **Example:** Consider the below BST

Binary Search Tree Demo
https://www.youtube.com/watch?v=cv_KDQzZpHs
Animation
Binary Search Tree Operations
https://www.cs.usfca.edu/~galles/visualization/BST.html

3. AVL Tree

51. AVL tree is a height balanced binary search tree . A binary search tree is said top be an AVL tree if the balancing factor of the tree is either 0 ,1 0r-1.

    Balancing factor= $h_L – h_R$

    Where h_L is the height of the left sub-tree and h_R is the height of the right sub-tree.

    Named after their inventor Adelson, Velski & Landis, AVL trees are height balancing binary search tree.
52. Node representation of AVL tree
53. Node is similar to a binary search tree, the only difference is an extra data filed representing the balancing factor is included in the node structure.

```
struct node
{
int info;
```

```
int balance;
struct node *lchild; struct node *rchild;
};
```

3.4.3.2 Operations on AVL Tree

54. **Insertion**
5. **Deletion**
5. **Traversal**
6.

7. Insertion
8. When insertion operations are performed on an AVL tree, the tree may loose its AVL tree property . To restore the AVL tree property different rotations are performed based on the imbalance as shown below

Algorithm

9. Perform normal binary search insertion operation
10. After insertion
11. n find the balancing factor at each node.
12. If balancing factors are 1,0 and -1 then no need to perform rotations the tree is AVL tree.
13. Else

    a. Starting from the point of insertion identify the first invalid balancing factor
    b. From the point traverse two edges towards the inserted node

14. If path traversed is LL perform RR rotation (single rotation)

If path traversed is RR perform LL rotation (single rotation) If path traversed is LR perform RL rotation (double rotation)

If path traversed is RL perform LR rotation (double rotation)

Example: Construct an AVL tree with the elements 14, 17, 11, 7, 4, 13,19 and 18.

Successive insertion operations will construct the AVL tree as shown below

Insert 19

Deletion in AVL Tree

Deleting an element is similar to binary search tree, that is it involves three cases no child case, one child case and two child case.

After deleting we check the balancing factor at each node after deletion. If there are any invalid balancing factors we perform the rotations to restore the AVL tree properties.

Example: Consider deleting the elements 7, 11, 14, 17 from the below AVL tree

AVL Tree rotation
https://www.youtube.com/watch?v=kdfxT8ed4Ww
Animation
AVL Tree Operations
https://www.cs.usfca.edu/~galles/visualization/AVLtree.html

3.4.4.2 B+ Trees

A B+ tree is a variant of a B tree which stores sorted data in a way that allows for efficient insertion, retrieval, and removal of records, each of which is identified by a key. While a B tree can store both keys and records in its interior nodes, a B+ tree, in contrast, stores all the records at the leaf level of the tree; only keys are stored in the interior nodes.

of order 3.

B+ trees store data only in the leaf nodes. All other nodes (internal nodes) are called index nodes or i-nodes and store index values. Figure 3.13 shows a B+ tree

Figure 3.13. B+ Tree

15. Comparison between B-Tree and B+-Tree
16.

Sl.NO	**B-Tree**	**B+ Tree**
1.	Data is stored in internal or leaf nodes	Data is stored only in leaf nodes
2.	Search keys are not repeated	Stores redundant search keys
3.	Searching takes mare time as data may be found in a leaf node or internal node	Searching data is very easy as the data can be found only at leaf nodes
4.	Deletion of non-leaf nodes is very complicated	Data is very simple as data lie only at leaf nodes
5.	Insertion takes more time and it is not predictable sometimes.	Insertion is easier and the results are always the same.
6.	Leaf nodes are not linked with each other.	Leaf nodes are linked as a linked list.
7.	The structure and operations are complicated	The structure and operations are simple

17. Inserting a New element in a b+ Tree
18. A new element is simply added in the leaf node if there is space for it. But if the data node in the tree where insertion has to be done is full, then that node is split into two nodes. This calls for adding a new index value in the parent index node so that future queries can arbitrate between the two new nodes.

    Algorithm

    Step 1: Insert the new node as the leaf node.

    Step 2: If the leaf node overflows, split the node and copy the middle element to next index node.

    Step 3: If the index node overflows, split that node and move the middle element to next index page.

Example: Consider the B+ tree of order 4 given and insert 33 in it.

Step-1 : Inserting 33

Step-2: Splitting the leaf node

Step-3 : Splitting the index

19. Deleting an element from a b+ Tree
20. As in B trees, deletion is always done from a leaf node. If deleting a data element leaves that node empty, then the neighbouring nodes are examined and merged with the underfull node. This process calls for the deletion of an index value from the parent index node which, in turn, may cause it to become empty. Similar to the insertion process, deletion may cause a merge-delete wave to run from a leaf node all the way up to the root.

Algorithm

Step 1: Delete the key and data from the leaves.

Step 2: If the leaf node underflows, merge that node with the sibling and delete the key in between them.

Step 3: If the index node underflows, merge that node with the sibling and move down the key in between them.

Example: Consider the B+ tree of order 4 given below and delete node 15 from it.

Step-1: Deleting 15

Step-2: Leaf node under flow so merge with left sibling and remove key 15

Step-3: Now index node under flow occurs, so merge with sibling and delete the node

21. Searching a node in a B+ Tree
22. Perform a binary search on the records in the current node.
23. If a record with the search key is found, then return that record.
24. If the current node is a leaf node and the key is not found, then report an unsuccessful search.

25. Otherwise, follow the proper branch and repeat the process.
26. Example:
27. **Advantages Of B+ Trees**
28. We can fetch records in an equal number of disk accesses.
29. Compared to the B tree, the height of the B+ tree is less and remains balanced.
30. We use keys for indexing.
31. Data in the B+ tree can be accessed sequentially or directly as the leaf nodes are arranged in a linked list.
32. Search is faster as data is stored in leaf nodes only and as a linked list.

33.

B+ Tree Insertions
https://www.youtube.com/watch?v=h6Mw7_S4ai0
Animation
B + Tree Operations
https://www.cs.usfca.edu/~galles/visualization/BPlusTree.html

5. Binary Heap

35. A binary heap is a binary tree in which satisfies the following two properties
36. It's a Complete Binary tree
37. Heap property i.e. its either Max-heap property or Min-Heap
38. Max-Heap: Elements at every node will be either greater than or equal to the element at its left and right child. Thus, the root has the greatest key value. Such a heap is called a **max-heap.**

    If B is a child of A, then key(A) >= key(B)

    Min-Heap:Elements at every node will be either less than or equal to the element at its left and right child. Thus, the root has the lowest key value. Such a heap is called **a min-heap**.

    If B is a child of A, then key(A) < = key(B)

Heaps (also known as partially ordered trees) are a very popular data structure for implementing priority queues. Figure 3.14 shows a binary max-heap and min-heap

Figure 3.14 : Binary Heap

Since a heap is defined as a complete binary tree, all its elements can be stored sequentially in an array.

1. Inserting a New Element in a Binary Heap

40. Consider a max heap H with n elements. Inserting a new value into the heap is done using the below algorithm

Algorithm:

Step-1. Add the new value at the bottom of H in such a way that H is still a
complete binary tree but not necessarily a heap.

Step-2. Let the new value rise to its appropriate place in H so that H now becomes a heap as well. **This operation is known as heapify.**

Example: Consider the max heap given below and insert 99 in it.

Step-1: Inserting 99

Satisfying the Complete binary tree property 99 is inserted as a right child to 27

Step-2: Hepify operation

Compare 99 with its parent node value. If it is less than its parent's value, then the new node is in its appropriate place and H is a heap. If the new value is greater than that of its

parent's node, then swap the two values. Repeat the whole process until H becomes a heap as shown below

Example : Build a max heap H from the given set of numbers: 45, 36, 54, 27, 63,

72, 61,

and 18. Also draw the memory representation of the heap.

The memory representation is shown below

2. Deleting an Element from Heap

42. Consider a max heap H having n elements. An element is always deleted from the root of the heap. So, deleting an element from the heap is done in the following three steps:

Algorithm:

Step-1 Replace the root node's value with the last node's value so that H is still a complete binary tree but not necessarily a heap.

Step-2 Delete the last node.

Step-3 Sink down the new root node's value so that H satisfies the heap property. In this step, interchange the root node's value with its child node's value (whichever is largest among its children).

Example: Perform deletion operation on the below heap

Here the value of root node = 54 and the value of the last node = 11. So, replace 54 with 11 and delete the last node.

Applications of Binary Heap

43. Heaps are used in many famous algorithms such as Dijkstra's algorithm for finding the shortest path, the heap sort sorting algorithm.
44. Heap is used for implementing priority queues.
45. Essentially, heaps are the data structure you want to use when you want to be able to access the maximum or minimum element very quickly.

46.

Heap sort
https://www.youtube.com/watch?v=4TBlNn4PJ0I
Animation
Min Heap Operations
https://www.cs.usfca.edu/~galles/visualization/Heap.ht
ml

47. M-Way Search Tree
48. M-way search tree has M – 1 values per node and M sub- Pointer to left sub-tree trees. In such a tree, M is called the degree of the tree.

Note that in a binary search tree M = 2, so it has one value and two sub-trees. In other words, every internal node of an M-way search tree consists of pointers to M sub-trees and contains M – 1 keys, where M > 2. The structure of an M-way search tree node is shown in Figure 3.11

Figure 3.11: Structure of M-way search Tree

In the structure shown, P_0, P_1, ...,P_n are pointers to the node's sub-trees and K_0, K_1, ...,K_{n-1} are the key values of the node. All the key values are stored in ascending order.

1. B-Tree

A B tree is a specialized M-way tree. A B tree of order m can have a maximum of m– 1 keys and m pointers to its sub-trees. A B tree may contain a large number of key

values and pointers to sub-trees.

A B tree is designed to store sorted data and allows search, insertion, and deletion operations to be performed in logarithmic amortized time.

49. Properties of B-Tree
50. Every node in the B tree has a maximum of m children.
51. Every node in the B tree except the root node and leaf nodes has a minimum of m/2 children.
52. The root node has at least two children if it is not a terminal (leaf) node.
53. All leaf nodes are at the same level.
54.

Figure 3.12 : B-Tree of order 4

55. Inserting a New element in a B-Tree
56. In a B tree, all insertions are done at the leaf node level. A new value is inserted in the B tree using the algorithm given below.
57. Search the B tree to find the leaf node where the new key value should be inserted.
58. If the leaf node is not full, that is, it contains **less than m–1 key values**, then insert the new element in the node keeping the node's elements ordered.
59. If the **leaf node is full**, that is, the leaf node already contains m–1 key values, then

   a. insert the new value in order into the existing set of keys,
   b. split the node at its median into two nodes
   c. push the median element up to its parent's node. If the parent's node is already full, then split the parent node by following the same steps.

60. Example:
61. Look at the B tree of order 5 given below and insert 8, 9, 39, and 4 into it.

Inserting 8

Inserting 9

Inserting 39

We have easily inserted 8 and 9 in the tree because the leaf nodes were not full. But now, the node in which 39 should be inserted is already full as it contains four values. Here we split the nodes to form two separate nodes. But before splitting, arrange the key values in order (including the new value). The ordered set of values is given as 21, 27, 36, 39, and 42. The median value is 36, so push 36 into its parent's node and split the leaf nodes.

62. Deleting an Element From B-Tree
63. Deletion is also performed at the leaf nodes. The node which is to be deleted can either be a leaf node or an internal node. Following algorithm needs to be followed in order to delete a node from a B tree.

Case-1: Deleting a Leaf Node

64. Locate the leaf node.
65. If there are more than m/2 keys in the leaf node then delete the desired key from the node.
66. If the leaf node doesn't contain m/2 keys then complete the keys by taking the element from eight or left sibling.

   i. If the left sibling contains more than m/2 elements then push its largest element up to its parent and move the intervening element down to the

67. node where the key is deleted.

   ii. If the right sibling contains more than m/2 elements then push its smallest element up to the parent and move intervening element down to the node where the key is deleted.

69.

70. If neither of the sibling contain more than m/2 elements then create a new leaf node by joining two leaf nodes and the intervening element of the parent node. 5.If parent is left with less than m/2 nodes then, apply the above process on the parent too.
71. **Case-2: Deleting Internal Node**

    If the node which is to be deleted is an internal node, then replace the node with its in-order successor or predecessor. Since, successor or predecessor will always be on the leaf node hence, the process will be similar as the node is being deleted from the leaf node.
72. 180, and 72 from it

    Example: Consider the following B tree of order 5 and delete values 93, 201,
73. Deleting 93

Deleting 201
Deleting 180

74. Searching a node in a B-Tree
75. Perform a binary search on the records in the current node.
76. If a record with the search key is found, then return that record.
77. If the current node is a leaf node and the key is not found, then report an unsuccessful search.
78. Otherwise, follow the proper branch and repeat the process.
79. **Example:** Searching for the element 27 in the below B Tree

Advantages:

80. Lack of redundant storage (but only marginally different).
81. Some searches are faster (key may be in non-leaf node).
82. **Disadvantages:**
83. Leaf and non-leaf nodes are of different size (complicates storage)
84. Deletion may occur in a non-leaf node (more complicated)

85.

B Tree example
https://www.youtube.com/watch?v=coRJrcIYbF4
Animation
B Tree Operations
https://www.cs.usfca.edu/~galles/visualization/BTree.html

PART A : Q & A : UNIT – IV

Questions and Answers

Define non-linear data structure.

Every data item is attached to several other data items in a way that is specific for reflecting relationships. The data items are not arranged in a sequential structure.

Ex: Trees, Graphs

Define Tree.

A tree is a collection of nodes. The collection can be empty, which is sometimes denoted as A. Otherwise, a tree consists of a distinguished node r, called the root, and zero or more (sub) trees T1, T2, . . . , Tk, each of whose roots are connected by a directed edge to r.

Define Path.

A path from node n_1 to n_k is defined as a sequence of nodes n_1, n_2, . . . , n_k such that n_i is the parent of n_{i+1} for 1 i < k. The length of this path is the number of edges on the path, namely k -1. There is a path of length zero from every node to itself.

Note : In a tree there is exactly one path from the root to each node.

What do you mean by tree traversal? Mention its types.

Tree traversal (also known as tree search and walking the tree) is a form of graph traversal and refers to the process of visiting (checking and/or updating) each node in a tree data structure, exactly once. Such traversals are classified by the order in which the nodes are visited. Pre order Traversal ? Root, Left subtree, Right subtree In order Traversal ? Left subtree, Root, Right subtree Post order Traversal ? Left subtree, Right subtree, Root

PART A : Q & A : UNIT – IV

Questions and Answers

Give some applications of Trees. Implementing the file system of several operating systems.

Evaluation of arithmetic expression. Set representation.

Gaming/Decision making problems.

What is a binary tree?

A binary tree is a tree in which no node can have more than two children. A property of a binary tree is that the depth of an average binary tree is considerably smaller than n. The average depth of the special type of binary tree, namely the binary search tree, is O(log n).

Define node, degree, siblings, depth/height, level. Node: A node is an item of information with branches to other items.

Degree: The number of subtrees of a node is called is degree.

Siblings: The children of the same parent is said to be siblings.

Level: The level of a node is defined recursively by assuming the level of the root to be one and if a node is at level l, then its children at level l+1.

Depth/Height: The depth/height of a tree is defined to be the level of a node which is maximum.

In what ways a binary tree can be represented?

Array representation Linked list representation

What do you mean by binary search tree?

The property that makes a binary tree into a binary search tree is that for every node, X, in the tree, the values of all the keys in the left subtree are smaller than the key value in X, and the values of all the keys in the right subtree are larger than the key value in X.

PART A : Q & A : UNIT – IV

Questions and Answers

State the advantages and disadvantage of array representation of a binary tree.

Advantages:

Storage method is easy and can be easily implemented in

arrays

When the location of a parent/child node is known, other one can be determined easily

It requires static memory allocation so it is easily implemented in all programming language.

Disadvantage:

Insertions and deletions in a node take an excessive amount of processing time due to data movement up and down the array.

State the advantage and disadvantage of linked list representation of a binary tree.

Advantage :

Insertions and deletions in a node involve no data movement except the rearrangement of pointers, hence less processing time.

Disadvantage :

Given a node structure, it is difficult to determine its parent node

Memory spaces are wasted for storing null pointers for the nodes, which have one or no sub-trees

It requires dynamic memory allocation, which is not possible in some programming language

Write a note of expression tree.

The leaves of an expression tree are operands, such as constants or variable names, and the other nodes contain operators. This particular tree is a binary tree, because all of the operations are binary. It is possible for nodes to have more than two children and to have only one child, as is the case with the unary minus operator.

PART A : Q & A : UNIT – IV

Questions and Answers

Mention the characteristics of a threaded binary tree.

A binary tree is threaded by making all right child

pointers that would normally be null point to the in-order successor of the node (if it exists), and all left child pointers that would normally be null point to the in-order predecessor of the node.

Define balanced search tree.

Balanced search tree have the structure of binary tree and obey binary search tree properties with that it always maintains the height as O(log n) by means of a special kind of rotations. Eg. AVL, Splay, B-tree.

Define AVL tree.

An empty tree is height balanced. If T is a non-empty binary tree with TL and TR as its left and right subtrees, then T is height balanced if TL and TR are height balanced.

$| hL - hR | \leq 1$. Where hL and hR are the height of TL and TR respectively.

What do you mean by rotation in an AVL tree? Manipulation of tree pointers is centered at the pivot node to bring the tree back into height balance. The visual effect of this pointer manipulation so to rotate the sub tree whose root is the pivot node. This operation is referred as AVL rotation.

List out the rotations of the AVL trees.

Single rotation ? Right rotation, Left rotation

Double rotation ? Right-Left rotation, Left-Right rotation

What are the drawbacks of AVL trees?

The drawbacks of AVL trees are

Frequent rotations

The need to maintain balances for the tree's nodes Overall complexity, especially of the deletion operation.

PART A : Q & A : UNIT – IV

Questions and Answers

What are the properties of a B-tree?

A B-tree of order m is a tree with the following structural properties:

The root is either a leaf or has between 2 and m

children.

All nonleaf nodes (except the root) have between m/2 and m children.

All leaves are at the same depth. All data is stored at the leaves

What is a heap?

A heap is a partially ordered data structure, and can be defined as a binary tree assigned to its nodes, one key per node, provided the following two conditions are met

The tree's shape requirement-The binary tree is essentially complete, that is all the leaves are full except possibly the last level, where only some rightmost leaves will be missing.

The parental dominance requirement-The key at each node is greater that or equal to the keys of its children

PART B QUESTIONS: UNIT – IV

86. Construct AVL trees with 3,1,4,5,9,2,8,7,0 into an initially empty tree. Write code for insertion. (13)
87. AVL insertion: 43, 11, 69, 72, 30. Delete 11, 72. Draw the structure of tree after every operation. (13)
88. Define AVL tree and starting with an empty AVL search tree, insert the following
89. elements in the given order: 2, 1, 4, 5, 9, 3, 6, 7. Then delete 1, 6 and 9 in
    order. (10)
90. Explain AVL rotations with a suitable example. (6)
91. Construct B-Tree with order m=3, for 2, 3, 7, 9, 5, 6, 4, 8, 1 and delete 4, 6. Show the tree in performing all operations. (7)
92. What is a B-tree? Mention the properties that a B-tree holds. (6)
93. Construct B+Tree with order m=3, for 2, 3, 7, 9, 5, 6, 4, 8, 1 and delete 4, 6.
94. Show the tree in performing all operations. (7)
95. Construct a BST by inserting 30,10,4,19,62,35,28,73 into an initially empty tree. Show the results of splaying the nodes 4, 62 one after other of the constructed tree. (10).
96. Insert 27, 17, 19, 20, 24, 12, 11, 10, 14, 18, delete min in an initially empty
97. binomial heap. (6)
98. For the given binary tree, write required routine &perform the different types of traversals. (13)
99. Applications of trees
100. Represent organization
101. Represent computer file systems
102. Networks to find best path in the Internet
103. Chemical formulas representation
104. Ordered storage to be used in binary search
105. Decision trees

106. Encoding
107. Telephone exchanges used a tree hierarchy to find the actual target phone when dialing a phone number, for example. It is again not a binary tree, but a "decimal" tree with 10 nodes coming off each individual node.
108. Applications of Binary Search Tree
109. Used in many search applications where data is constantly entering/leaving, such as the map and set objects in many languages' libraries. Binary Space Partition -
110. Used in almost every 3D video game to determine what objects need to be rendered.

Applications of AVL tree

111. Each IP packet sent by an Internet host is stamped with a 16-bit id that must be unique for that source-destination pair. Linux kernel uses an AVL tree (height balanced) indexed by IP address. Hashing would be faster, but want to avoid
112. attacker sending IP packets with worst-case inputs.

REAL TIME APPLICATIONS: UNIT - IV

113. Store hierarchical data, like folder structure, organization structure, XML/HTML data.
114. Binary Search Tree is a tree that allows fast search, insert, delete on a sorted
115. data. It also allows finding closest item
116. Heap is a tree data structure which is implemented using arrays and used to implement priority queues.
117. B-Tree and B+ Tree : They are used to implement indexing in databases.
118. Syntax Tree: Used in Compilers.
119. K-D Tree: A space partitioning tree used to organize points in K dimensional space.
120. Trie: Used to implement dictionaries with prefix lookup.
121. Suffix Tree : For quick pattern searching in a fixed text.
122. Spanning Trees and shortest path trees are used in routers and bridges respectively in computer networks
123. As a workflow for compositing digital images for visual effect
124. PRESCRIBED TEXT BOOKS & REFERENCE BOOKS

Text Books

1. Michael T. Goodrich, Roberto Tamassia, and Michael H. Goldwasser, "Data Structures & Algorithms in Python", John Wiley & Sons Inc., 2013 2. Lee, Kent D., Hubbard, Steve, "Data Structures and Algorithms with Python" Springer Edition 2015

Reference Books

125. Rance D. Necaise, "Data Structures and Algorithms Using Python", John Wiley &
126. Sons, 2011
127. Aho, Hopcroft, and Ullman, "Data Structures and Algorithms", Pearson Education, 1983.
128. Thomas H. Cormen, Charles E. Leiserson, Ronald L. Rivest, and Clifford Stein, "Introduction to Algorithms", Second Edition, McGraw Hill, 2002. 4. Mark Allen Weiss, "Data Structures and Algorithm Analysis in C++", Fourth Edition, Pearson Education, 2014
129.

Additional Reference Books

1. Data Structures and Algorithms Made Easy: Data Structures and Algorithmic Puzzles by Narasimha Karumanchi , Careermonk Publications, 5th edition, 2017

Thank you

REAL TIME APPLICATIONS: UNIT - IV

Thank you

www.ingramcontent.com/pod-product-compliance
Ingram Content Group UK Ltd.
Pitfield, Milton Keynes, MK11 3LW, UK
UKHW061706190726
13853UKWH00008B/2424